T O :

FROM:

ONE

SHINING

MOMENT

DAVID BARRETT

RUTLEDGE HILL PRESS | NASHVILLE, TENNESSEE
A DIVISION OF THOMAS NELSON PUBLISHERS | www.ThomasNelson.com

Dedicated to Tracy, Esther, and Claire - Thank you.

Special thanks: Deb, Will, Rob, and Glenn whose belief made it possible, the musicians, Armen, Doug, Scott, Mike, Bryan, Tom C., Mom, Mark, Jim N., and my friends at CBS Sports, Greg S. and my friends at the NCAA, and all those whose talent shines for us all.

Copyright © 2006 by David Barrett

Published by Rutledge Hill Press, a Division of Thomas Nelson, Inc., P.O. Box 141000, Nashville, Tennessee 37214.

Rutledge Hill Press books may be purchased in bulk for educational, business, fund-raising, or sales promotional use. For information, please e-mail SpecialMarkets@ThomasNelson.com.

1-4016-0244-4

Printed in Mexico
06 07 08 09 10 RRD 5 4 3 2

ONE SHINING MOMENT

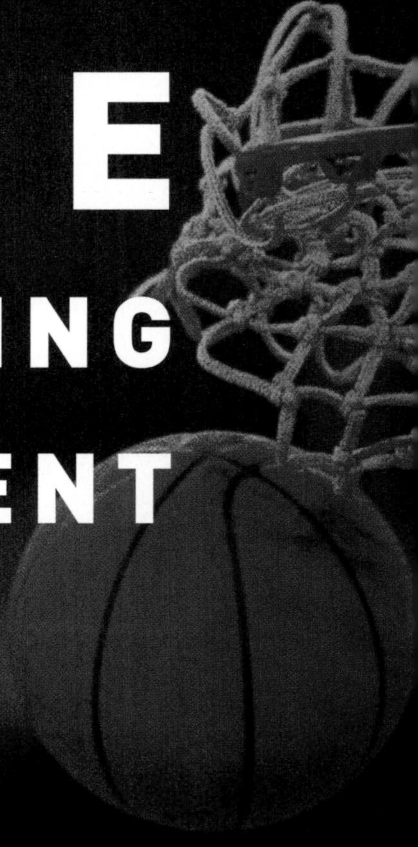

The ball is tipped
And there you are
You're running for your life
You're a shooting star

And all the years
No one knows
Just how hard you worked
But now it shows . . .

(In) One Shining Moment, It's All on the Line
One Shining Moment, There Frozen in Time

But time is short
And the road is long
In the blinking of an eye
Ah, that moment's gone

And when it's done
Win or lose
You always did your best
Cuz inside you knew (that) . . .

One Shining Moment,
You Reached Deep Inside
One Shining Moment,
You Knew You Were Alive

Feel the beat of your heart
Feel the wind in your face
It's more than a contest
It's more than a race.

And when it's done
Win or lose
You always did your best
Cuz inside you knew (that) . . .

One Shining Moment,
You Reached for the Sky
One Shining Moment, You Knew
One Shining Moment,
You Were Willing to Try
One Shining Moment

I was a writer-reporter working at Sports Illustrated in New York when David Barrett called to say he had written this song—something special, he thought. We were high school athletic rivals turned old friends, good friends. Send it along. Be happy to listen, I said.

From there, well, things moved rather quickly: From the first notes of the piano prelude to the first words ("The ball is tipped . . .") somehow, simply, poignantly, David had captured the purity and passion of college basketball. I sent the tape to a friend at CBS Sports. He called back saying as soon as he hit "play" on his machine, people rushed into his office to listen, to say, "this is what we've been searching for."

The year was 1987. This year marks the 20th anniversary of "One Shining Moment." Over those years it has not only closed our coverage of the March Madness, it has become the signature song of CBS Sports. Today, it's nothing less than the most powerful sports anthem around . . . the perfect theme song for the purest play in sport.

For much of the last decade, I've had the pleasure of being on the court at the Final Four, waiting, anticipating the Moment when the first chords ring and the video montage rolls, watching our annual tribute to the tournament, the ultimate road coaches and players and fans will never forget.

For me "One Shining Moment" has come to personify what is simply good and decent in sport. It has inspired more dreams on more courts than a million pregame speeches. I hope that here on these pages, David's poetic gifts, his insights into life, may inspire you and your dreams. Your life . . . one shining moment at a time.

—**ARMEN KETEYIAN**, REPORTER, CBS AND HBO SPORTS

IF YOU HAVE A COPY OF THIS BOOK IN YOUR HANDS, IT PROBABLY MEANS ONE OF TWO THINGS:

Someone in your life believes in your dreams and is showing it with this book, which makes you a lucky person with an angel on your shoulder.
Or . . .
You have your dreams that you quietly pursue on your own, and are willing to take the risks, pay the price in walking that road by yourself. That's the path I know something about.

In either case, I genuinely hope that the words, the images, and the song contained here will serve as inspiration. As I was composing my ideas for this book, a faint pattern began to emerge from the mists. Over and over again these four themes found their voices . . .

THE DREAM, THE PREPARATION, THE MOMENT, THE WINGS

No matter your destination, these themes seem to speak to the soul as the equipment necessary for the journey. And while there are no guarantees in this world, they may very well help you find your own shining moment.

DB

THE BALL IS TIPPED

AND THERE YOU ARE

YOU'RE RUNNING FOR YOUR LIFE

YOU'RE A SHOOTING STAR

This is a world of dreams. Big dreams, secret dreams,

broken dreams, sweet dreams—dreams all the same. Some lead to making the team, some lead to having children, some dreams even establish a new nation—dreams all the same. This is a world of dreams. Some dream about being rich, some dream about just not being poor anymore, some dream without money . . . about God—dreams all the same. # This is a world of dreams.

Long before the finish line, long before the final buzzer, long before the artist's paint dries on the canvas, The dream comes first. Long before the opening note of the symphony, long before the thoroughbred colt rises on unsteady legs, long before the author's pen is raised to begin the book, The dream comes first.

A DREAM VIBRATES LIKE A FILAMENT IN A LIGHT BULB, SHEDDING LIGHT, ANIMAT

Like a child chasing summer fireflies first across the lawn and then, eyes rubbing onward

half found - he will be tested. He will win, he will lose. He will celebrate, he will des

THE DREAM COMES FIRST.

HE ARTIST, THE ATHLETE WITH A STRANGE ALCHEMY, A POWERFUL PASSION.

eam takes him by the hand and leads him deep into the wilderness. It is there - half lost,

nd if he is lucky - perhaps even wise - he might just discover his soul.   Ah . . . but . . .

AND ALL THE YEARS
NO ONE KNOWS
JUST HOW HARD YOU WORKED
BUT NOW IT SHOWS .

IN THE 1968 SUMMER OLYMPICS IN MEXICO CITY there was a long jumper from the USA named Bob Beamon. The sport of long jumping essentially means getting a good head of steam and then, well, jumping to see how far you can go. In Olympic conditions, the

BOB BEAMON'S

SHINING MOMENT

difference between winning and losing is a hair's breadth. That night Bob Beamon got running down the track and jumped out of the pit. He went two feet longer than the world record!

THEY HADN'T BUILT THE PIT BIG ENOUGH FOR THAT DREAM, THAT MOMENT.

And so we prepare. Like a fisherman, we mend our nets. Like a musician, we carefully restring our guitar. We shoot those extra free throws after practice; stay after school and ask the teacher about some detail in her lecture. We tinker till our bicycles are ready to race, our eyes ready to see, our fingers ready to perform, so when the moment comes, we are ready.

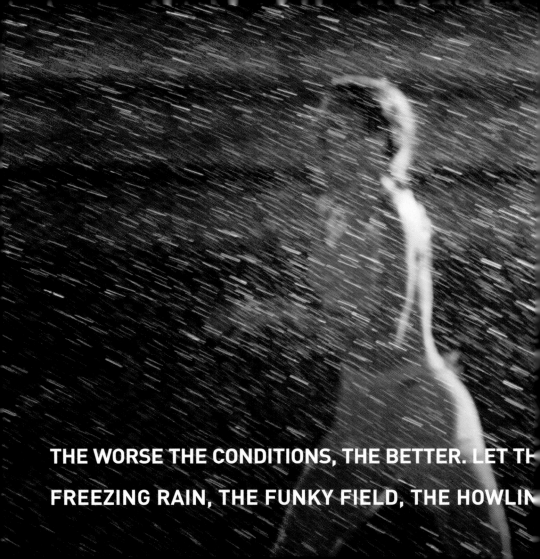

THE WORSE THE CONDITIONS, THE BETTER. LET TH

FREEZING RAIN, THE FUNKY FIELD, THE HOWLIN

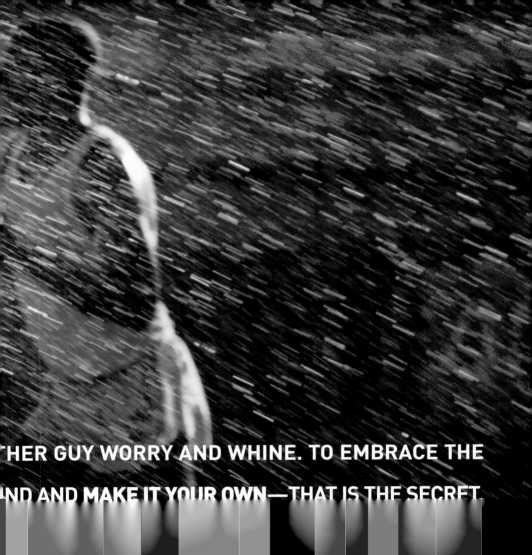

THER GUY WORRY AND WHINE. TO EMBRACE THE

ND AND **MAKE IT YOUR OWN**—THAT IS THE SECRET.

CONFIDENCE IS **THE GOAL**, NOT THE COTTON CAN

MUSCLES ON A LONG DISTANCE RUNNER. CONFIDENCE

SELF ESTEEM. CONFIDENCE GROWS LIKE WELL-FORMED

OT BEQUEATHED TO YOU. IT IS **EARNED** THROUGH TIME.

FINALLY, AFTER ALL THE QUIET DEDICATION,

BETTER YET, DEDICATION WITH BLOOD—DEVOTION

WHAT WAS ONCE A TENDER DREAM

FRAGILE AS A SPIDER WEB . . .

THAT YOU KEPT TO YOURSELF (FOR FEAR OF FEELING FOOLISH),

LIKE A COLT TRYING ITS FIRST STEPS ON WOBBLY LEGS

BUT THEN GROWING SURER

TAKES OFF TO GALLOP.

THIS RESTLESS STRIVING, **WHY?**

THIS ENDLESS PRACTICING, **WHY?** THIS ENDURING OF INJURIES, **WHY?**

BECAUSE **IT** SHOWS IN EVERY STROKE. **IT** SHOWS IN EVERY SHOT. **IT** SHOWS IN EVERY STRIDE

LIKE A ROCK WORN PERFECT BY THE WIND AND RAIN

THE "WHY" & THE "IT"

FIND EACH OTHER ON THE **INSIDE**.

THE ELEGANCE, THE GRACE, THE EASE OF PURPOSEFUL MOVEMENT SHOW UP ON THE **OUTSIDE**

AND THE DELICATE DANCE BETWEEN THE TWO AND THE DREAM . . .

THERE LIES THE WONDER.

KATE JOHNSON'S

SHINING MOMENT

IT IS VERY LIKELY THAT YOU HAVE NEVER HEARD OF KATE JOHNSON. That is, of course, unless you are a fan of rowing, which by any standard is one of the most demanding sports in the Olympics. She rowed through college at the University of Michigan and was picked to try out for the 2004 Olympic team. Quite an honor for the pride of Portland, Oregon. While trying to make the team, she fell into self-doubt and her performances showed it. The same body, the same mind, but the heart wondered. She might not have made

THE DREAM   THE PREPARATI

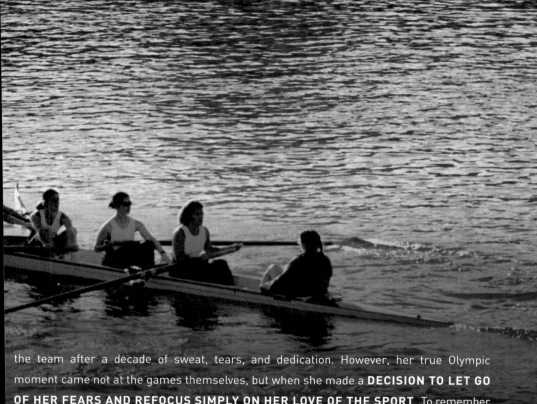

the team after a decade of sweat, tears, and dedication. However, her true Olympic moment came not at the games themselves, but when she made a **DECISION TO LET GO OF HER FEARS AND REFOCUS SIMPLY ON HER LOVE OF THE SPORT**. To remember the spirit of **WHY** over the mechanics of **HOW**. So when her boat crossed the finish line for an Olympic silver medal in Athens, it wasn't just the medal they hung around her neck that brought her joy, it was the belief in her heart.

THE   MOMENT   THE   WINGS

(IN) ONE **SHINING** MOMENT,
IT'S ALL ON THE LINE
ONE SHINING MOMENT,
THERE FROZEN IN TIME

POISE IS A FORM OF GRACE. LIKE A BREE

THE BRANCHES BENDING. YOU DON'T ACTUALLY WITNE

SSING THROUGH THE LEAVES OF A TREE, YOU NOTICE

E WIND, BUT YOU KNOW THAT IT IS THERE.

PERSEVERANCE

The wind will not always be at your back . . . PERSEVERE.

The light will not always shine for you . . . PERSEVERE.

Those you love might not understand your dreams . . . PERSEVERE.

It may take more time than you planned (man plans, God laughs) . . . PERSEVERE

It is a winding road your heart has led you down with . . . PERSEVERANCE.

MISTAKES

You will certainly know them.

They are the unwelcome guests that linger.

But disappointment is necessary to learn humility.

HUMILITY IS NOT SURRENDER
It is the firm foundation from which to build anew.

GRIT: (NOUN) UNYIELDING COURAGE, INDOMITABLE SPIRIT

GRIT ONLY HAPPENS WHEN YOU ARE HOPELESSLY OVERMATCHED.

IT IS THEN YOU LET GO OF THE SCORE—

SET YOUR JAW, GET A BIT ORNERY—AND PLAY OUT OF PERSONAL PRIDE.

THAT IS GRIT.

THE ZONE

Ask any athlete about "the zone." It will bring a delicious smile.

Ask any musician and you will get the same look.

It is where **YOUR BODY, YOUR MIND, YOUR HEART—**

the game being played or the song being sung—all converge.

Transcendence . . . it is inspired presence

MAY YOU NEVER CONFUSE . . .

YOUR WATCH WITH YOUR TIME,
YOUR MONEY WITH YOUR RICHES,
WINNING WITH VICTORY

THE DISTANCE BETWEEN THESE THINGS IS
ALL THE DIFFERENCE IN THE WORLD.

STEFAN XIDAS'

SHINING MOMENT

IT WASN'T ALWAYS EASY for him to sing in front of people, let alone to the 40,000 or so that crowded into the stadium to watch the Chicago White Sox play that balmy August night. But sing he did. Stefan calmly walked out to the microphone behind home plate and began to sing our national anthem. At first he sang tentatively, then gaining confidence as he went along, he ended with a crescendo with the lyrics ". . . land of the free." With that line, the crowd exploded with wild applause that seemed to pour over Stefan like waves of joy. For seventeen years his dad and mom had raised him to be

UNAFRAID OF THE CHALLENGES

that come with having Down Syndrome, and at that place, at that time, their love and his voice merged in a moment of perfection.

THE DREAM   THE PREPARATION   THE MOMENT   THE WINGS

BUT TIME IS SHORT
AND THE ROAD IS LONG
IN THE BLINKING OF AN EYE
AH . . . THAT MOMENT'S GONE
AND WHEN IT'S DONE
WIN OR LOSE
YOU ALWAYS DID YOUR BEST
CUZ INSIDE YOU KNEW . . .

When I was a boy, around fourteen, I played on my junior high baseball team. I had lost my father to cancer the year before. My family was struggling to put things back together and I felt lost in the grey fog of it all. We were playing a school named Crary who led us by a run in the last inning. With a runner on base, I came up to bat. As I stepped into the batter's box, I looked back in the distance to see my grandfather sitting on a portable chair under an oak tree. **HE JUST WAS THERE**, without fanfare, without a word. I will carry that picture in my mind to my grave. I simply felt this sense of **I SEE YOU**, which is important to a lost fourteen year old boy. I took a couple of pitches before sending a line drive into the left field corner. After sliding into third base and dusting myself off, I looked back under that oak tree. He just gave a slight nod. **SURPRISING WHAT A SLIGHT NOD CAN DO FOR A YOUNG MAN**. I honestly can't tell you whether we won or lost that game, but I can tell you how wings feel.

WINGS

You have these wings.

You may not see them, but they are there

Sure as the ones painted on the ceiling of the Sistine Chapel.

You grow them day by day, practice by practice, note by note.

So now when you glide gracefully over the ice, extend perfectly to catch a fly ball,

hit every note in the concerto . . .

There may not be feathers, but there are wings.

You earned them.

FEEL THE BEAT OF YOUR HEART
FEEL THE WIND IN YOUR FACE.
IT'S MORE THAN A CONTEST.
IT'S MORE THAN A RACE.

There is a funky little gym in Flint, Michigan. From the outside it looks like a 1950s bomb shelter. The lighting inside is out of a grade B movie, while the rims are hopelessly gnarled from years of overuse and ESPN reenactments. **BUT IT IS A FACT: IF YOU "HAVE GAME", YOU SHOW UP AND PLAY HERE.** And so for years this is where some of the best players in America have learned the game and grit it takes before going off to college and then the pros. One of whom was Mateen Cleaves. He was a resident gym rat since he was a boy. And after all the endless pickup games were through—the trash talking lessons completed—he would stand alone in this gym shooting free throws, quietly singing a song to himself . . . "the ball is tipped, and there you are. . . . " Sometimes he would make up his own lyrics. But hearing that song after winning the NCAA basketball championship game was his dream.

Years later, after MSU defeated Florida in a very gritty final game in the 2000 NCAA Basketball Championship, Mateen returned to the court to play with a sprained ankle the size of a grapefruit (lessons from the gym). The players milled around the court hugging and waiting, waiting and hugging, looking up at the jumbo screen in anticipation . . . and the song begins: "The ball is tipped, and there you are . . . " **MATEEN LOOKS UP . . . UTTER JOY!**

THE DREAM   THE PREPARATION   THE MOMENT   THE WINGS

MATEEN CLEAVES'

SHINING MOMENT

In the end, you stand on the mountaintop with your arms stretched upward,

finger pointing to the sky. Your body is spent; your heart is on fire.

The game is over.

And as is almost always the case, someone won and someone lost.

Either way, both are joined together forever

by the striving, the passion . . . the moment.

And when the colors have all run,

And the paint has dried on the portrait of a game already turning into a memory,

Only those who

TAKE THE CHANCE

HAVE THE HEART

GIVE IT UP

ONLY THEY WILL UNIQUELY KNOW WHAT HAPPENS WHEN YOU PUT IT ALL ON THE LINE.

So when it is all said and done

And the confetti spills down from the rafters and unashamed embraces replace high fives,

TAKE A GOOD LOOK AROUND AND BASK IN YOUR SHINING MOMENT.

ONE SHINING MOMENT,
YOU REACHED FOR THE SKY
ONE SHINING MOMENT, YOU KNEW
ONE SHINING MOMENT,
YOU WERE WILLING TO TR
ONE SHINING MOMENT . . .

To those few who came before me to help clear the way, thank you.

To those few who follow, please learn to say the same . . .

thank you.